Hovercraft Headache

Marcy Schaaf

Dedication

To my brothers, Joe and Frank Schaaf,

Thank you for filling my life with laughter, adventures, and countless memories. Your boundless energy and fearless spirits have always been a source of inspiration and joy. From our childhood escapades to our grown-up adventures, the love and bond we share are unbreakable. This story is a tribute to the fun and love we share, and a reminder of the importance of brotherly love, listening, and always having each other's backs.

With all my heart
Your little sister
Marcy Schaaf

Copyright @ Marcy Schaaf 2024
Books By Schaaf
Hovercraft Headache

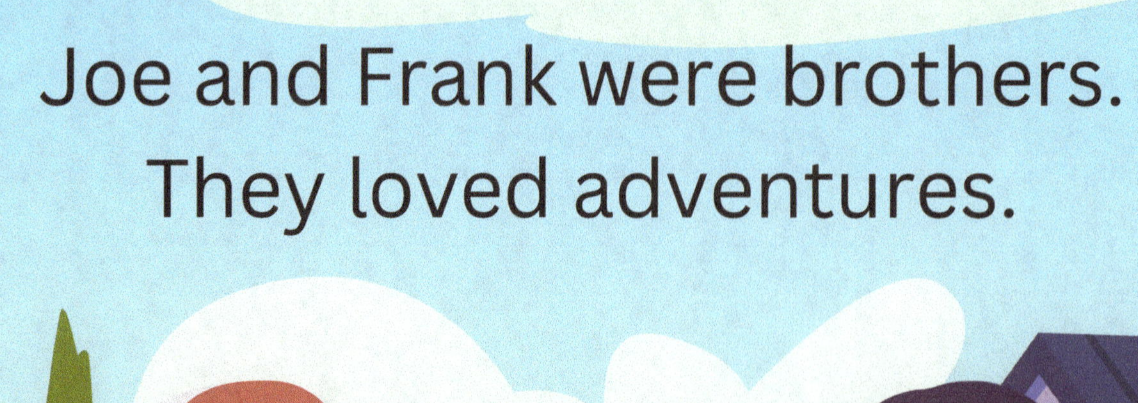

Joe and Frank were brothers.
They loved adventures.

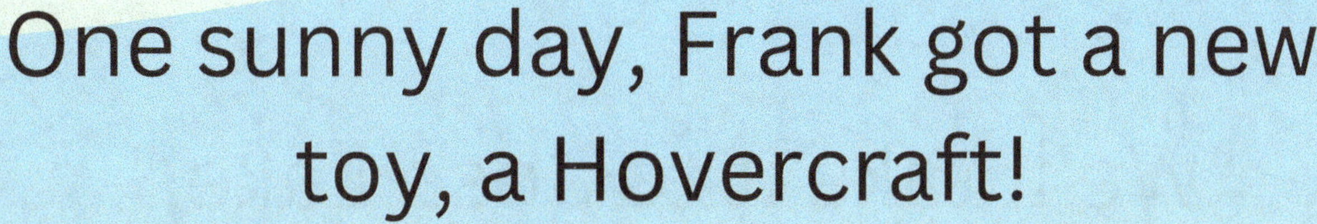

One sunny day, Frank got a new toy, a Hovercraft!

"We'll take it to Jose Lake,"
Frank said excitedly.

Frank began explaining how to use the Hovercraft.

But Joe was too excited.
He didn't listen.

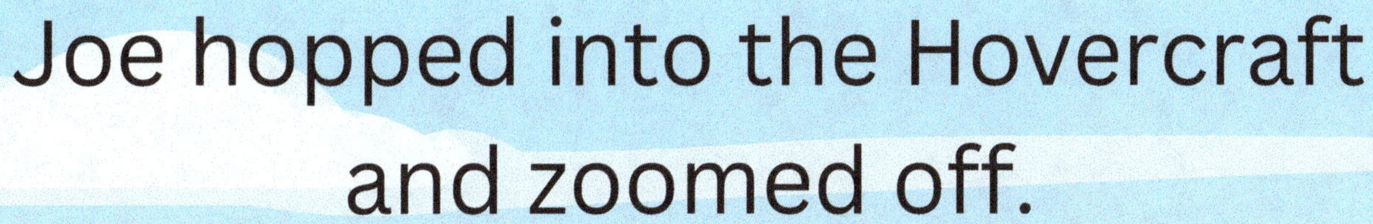

Joe hopped into the Hovercraft
and zoomed off.

He let go of the gas too quickly.

The Hovercraft stopped suddenly!

Joe flew over the steering wheel
and into the lake.

The Hovercraft kept moving, heading towards Joe!

It smacked Joe right in the head.
Ouch!

Frank saw everything from the shore.

He dove into the chilly water to save Joe.

Frank swam as fast as he could.

He reached Joe and helped him to shore.

Joe had a big lump on his head.

"I'm sorry, Frank," Joe said sadly.

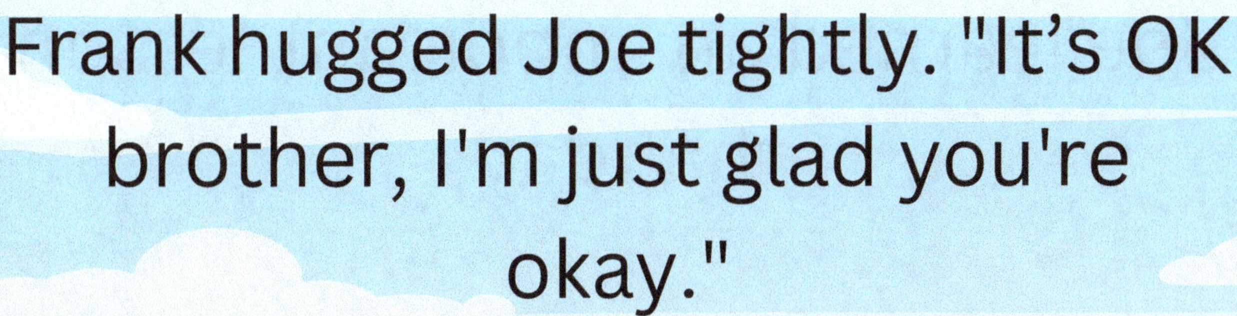

Frank hugged Joe tightly. "It's OK brother, I'm just glad you're okay."

Joe learned an important lesson
that day.

"Always listen to instructions,"
Frank said.

Joe nodded,
rubbing his sore head.

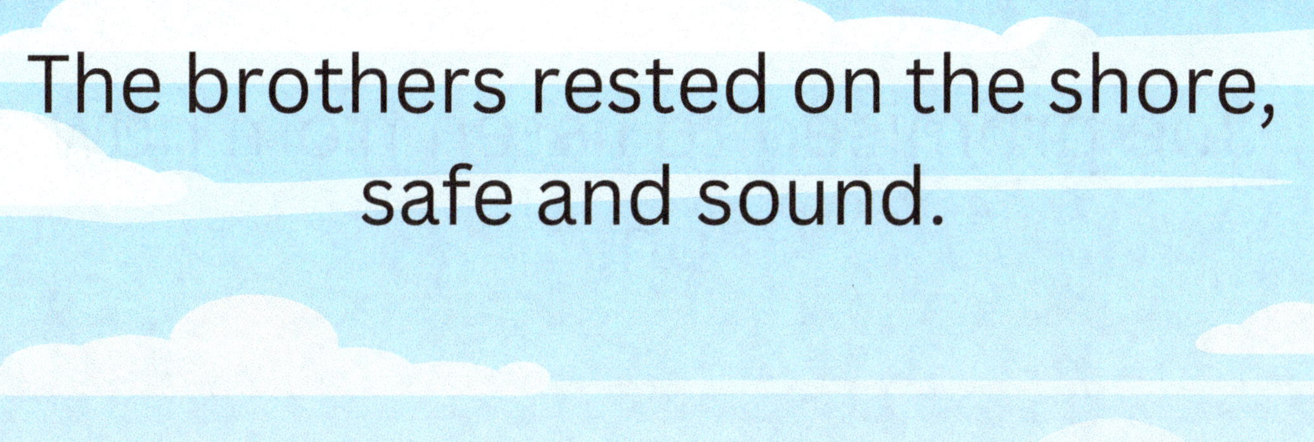

The brothers rested on the shore, safe and sound.

Joe promised to listen from now on.

Frank smiled. "We'll have more
fun this way."

The Hovercraft adventure
wasn't over yet.

They both took turns,
carefully this time.

Joe and Frank had a blast
on the lake.

Brotherly love and listening saved the day.

Moral of the story:
Listen to instructions or
get a lump on your head!

The End.

Books By Schaaf

www.BookBySchaaf.com

Find us at: